LIGHT
OF THE
SACRAMENTS

WORDS

Cory Heimann

◆

PICTURES

Tricia Dugat

Published by Word on Fire Spark, an imprint of
Word on Fire, Elk Grove Village, IL 60007
© 2024 by Word on Fire Catholic Ministries
Printed in the United States of America

Art direction by Nicolas Fredrickson and Rozann Lee
Editing by Haley Stewart

Special thanks to
Marie Heimann, Andy Bonjour, Erica Stein, and Sally Read

First printing, March 2024
ISBN: 978-1-68578-119-4

Library of Congress Control Number: 2023946692

Shine the light
behind the pages
with this symbol
in the corner!

Jesus is living, not stuck in a book,
Still shining now when we take a good look.
Light of the Sacraments! What does that mean?
Visible signs of His graces unseen.

Jesus went down to the river and said,
"John, would you pour water over my head?"
The Spirit appeared in the form of a dove.
The Father said, "This is my Son whom I love."

BE BAPTIZED

EVERY ONE OF YOU

IN THE NAME OF

JESUS CHRIST

ACTS 2:38

Over our heads holy water is poured,
Washing us clean with the grace of our Lord.
White garments show that God cleansed us of sin.
Candles are lit and Christ shines deep within.

RECONCILIATION

Jesus looked up at the roof and He saw
A man lowered down on a mat made of straw.
He said to the man who had paralyzed limbs,
"Stand up and walk! I forgive all your sins!"

WHOSE SINS

YOU
FORGIVE
ARE

FORGIVEN

JOHN 20:23

We all make mistakes and forget to do good,
Things that we'd go back and change if we could.
To Christ through the priest all our wrongs are confessed.
Free of our sins, with God's mercy we're blessed.

SOURCE SUMMIT

HOLY

EUCHARIST

Jesus sat down with His friends and broke bread,
"Eat of my body and you will be fed."
Taking the cup, as He raised it He said,
"Drink of this wine, it's the blood I will shed."

THIS IS

MY
BODY

LUKE 22:19

Coming to Mass where we join the Lord's feast,
The bread becomes Jesus with prayers from the priest.
This holy moment: when Heaven meets Earth,
Sharing a gift that's of infinite worth.

When Jesus ascended, His friends stuck together.
He sent them His Spirit, to guide them forever.
Faith in each heart and a flame on each head,
Strengthened to follow wherever He led.

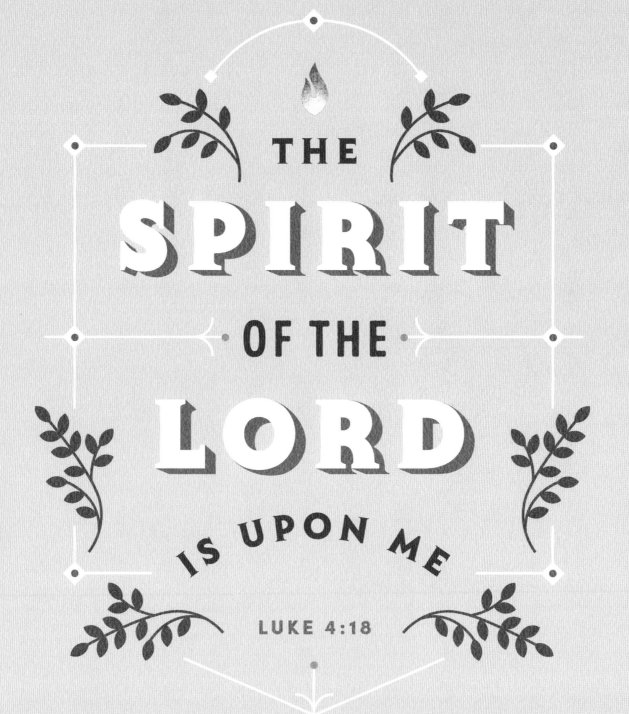

THE
SPIRIT
OF THE
LORD
IS UPON ME

LUKE 4:18

Anointed with oil we're given God's Spirit
To bravely go out in the world, and not fear it.
Rooted in grace and renewed in our zeal,
He strengthens our faith with a powerful seal!

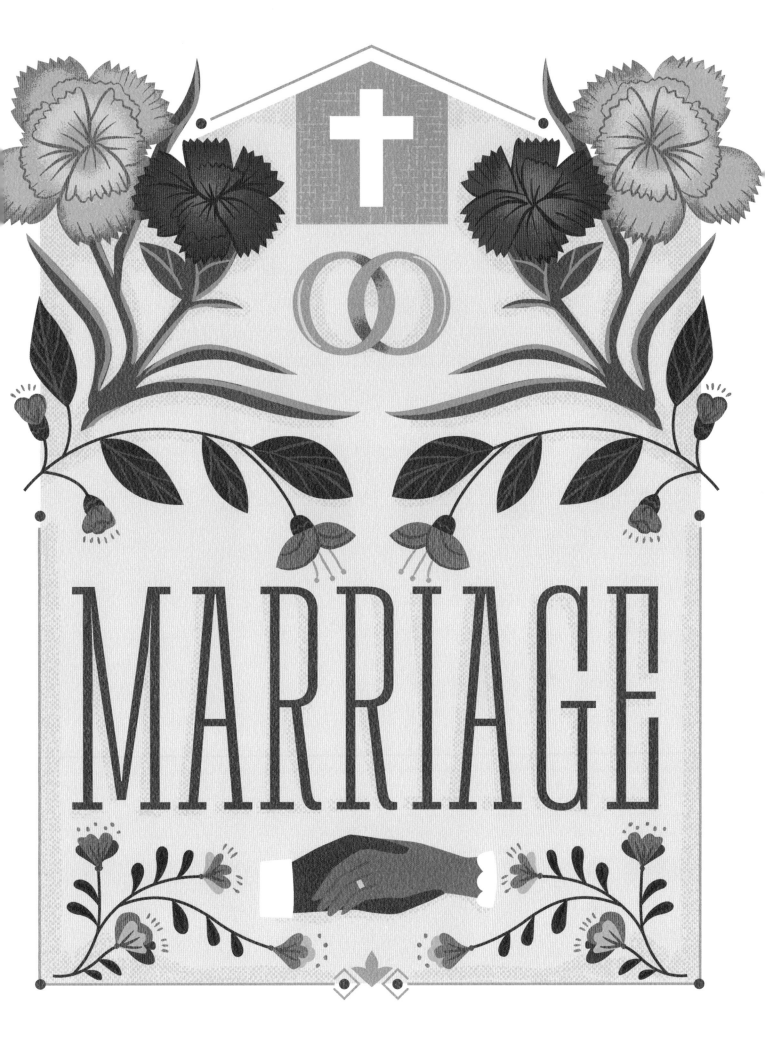

MARRIAGE

The moment when Jesus first showed His power:
A wedding in Cana—a most joyful hour!
Mary said, "Son, all the drinks have run dry!"
Water turned wine in the blink of an eye.

THEY ARE
NO LONGER
TWO, BUT
ONE
FLESH
MATTHEW 19:6

A wedding's the place where two souls become one.
A family is born, an adventure begun!
In sickness and health, in joy and in sorrow,
Loving like Christ, both today and tomorrow.

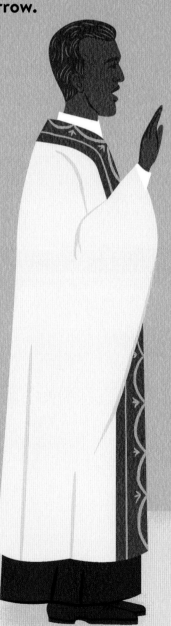

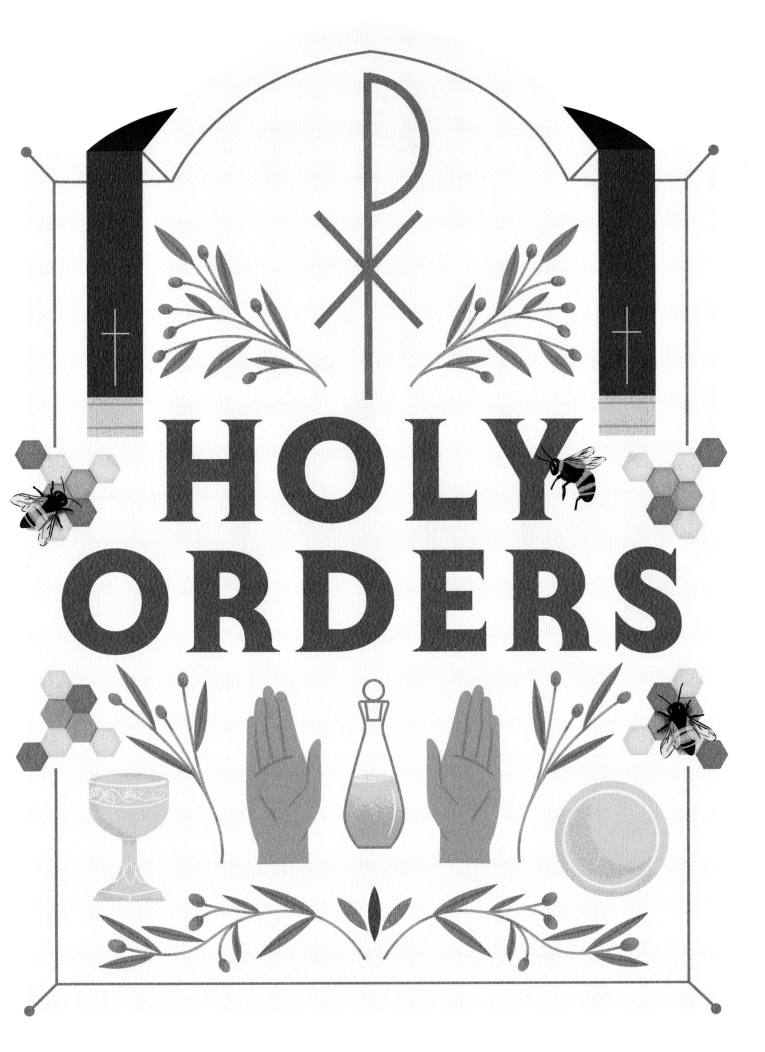

HOLY ORDERS

"Gather 'round, friends, for I must wash your feet,
They're dirty with dust—yes, even yours, Pete!"
Peter agreed to this humble endeavor.
Priesthood is serving God's people forever.

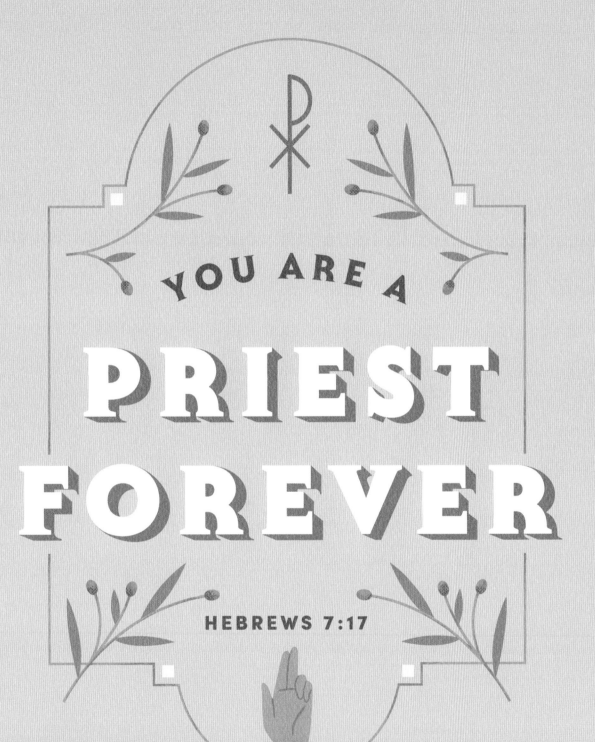

YOU ARE A

PRIEST
FOREVER

HEBREWS 7:17

When you're at Mass see the man at the altar,
Whether his name is Francisco or Walter,
We call him "Father," the priest in this place,
God's earthly vessel of fatherly grace.

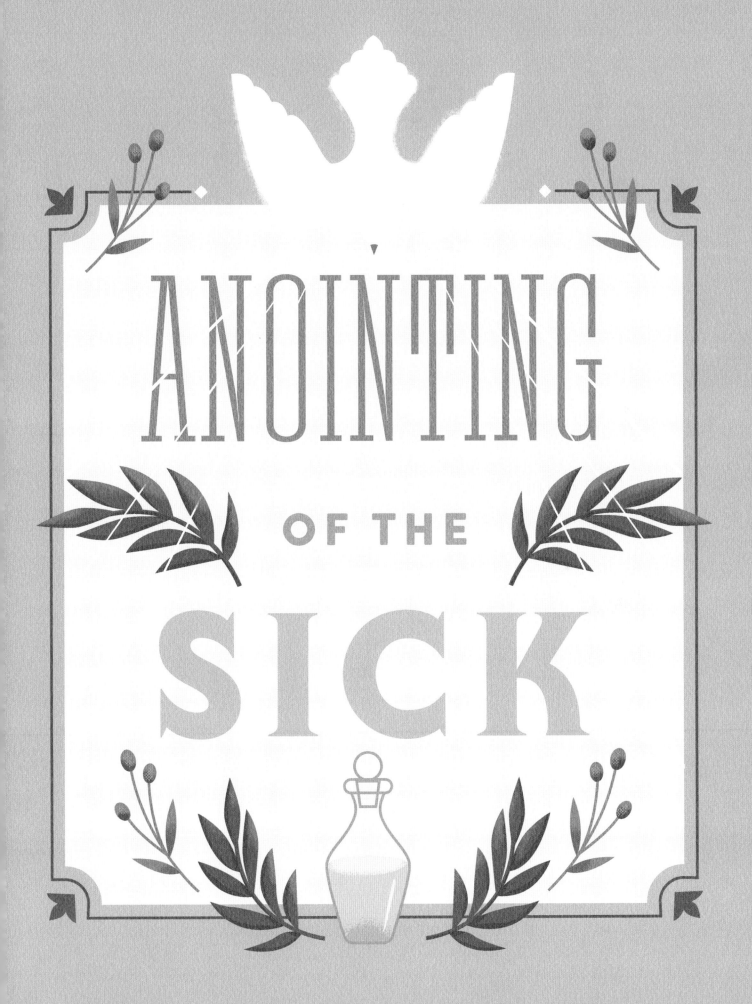

ANOINTING
OF THE
SICK

Jesus sent out all His friends, two by two,
Blessing with oil, curing more than a few.
When battling evil and healing the ill—
Anointing the sick—we are doing it still.

BE CURED

OF YOUR

AFFLICTION

MARK 5:34

Surgery's scheduled? You're really quite sick?
Anointing is offered to you super quick!
You could be one or one hundred and seven,
But grace is for healing and getting to heaven!

Grace of the Sacraments lights up your way.
What Christ did back then He is doing today:
Offering His love and imparting His grace,
Longing to give us His holy embrace.